Phyllis Limbacher

Eye Guess

A Foldout Guessing Game

ini Charlesbridge

I waddle on land, but I paddle in a puddle. With my wide, webbed feet, I can swim and dive. I open my eyes under water to look for food.

Can you guess who I am?

a duck

My home goes everywhere
I go. I pop inside when
I need to hide. I can play
peekaboo with you.

Can you guess who I am?

a turtle

My big eyes match my big mouth.

But all I ever say is

"Cro-o-ak. Cro-o-ak."

I love to eat a tasty bug.

Can you guess who I am?

I hide my eyes in a black fur mask. My little hands can snatch an egg from a nest or pick a berry from a branch. I like to go fishing as the sun goes down.

Can you guess who I am?

a frog

a raccoon

I have stripes, spots, pointed ears, and a stubby tail. I look like a big kitty cat, but I am not tame. I see very well in daylight or darkness.

Can you guess who I am?

a bobcat

I have tiny white feet, a long
tail, and twitchy whiskers.
My beady black eyes are
always watching for danger.
I make a soft nest of grass
and leaves in my burrow.

Can you guess who I am?

a mouse

I nap in a tree by day.

My eyes are wide and bright

at night. Even in the dark,

I can spy a little mouse below.

Can you guess whoooo I am?

an owl

My eyes glow in the shadows.

I travel with a pack of friends.

I like to howl at the moon.

Can you guess who I am?